TO: VINCENT

KEEP KNOCKING WALLS
DOWN

Thriving in a Disruptive World

KEEP PUSHING FORWARD!

THRIVE!

TO: VINCENT

KEEP KNOCKING WALLS
DOWN

KEEP PUSHING FORWARD!

THRIVE!

[signature]

Thriving in a Disruptive World

6 Critical Concepts for
Navigating the 21st Century

Julius Pryor III

*BOOK*LOGIX®
Alpharetta, GA

Paperback Edition January 2014

ISBN: 978-1-61005-451-5

Cover design by Blue Stranger X
www.bluestrangerx.com

Author photograph by Glenn Miller Film and Video Production
www.glennmillerfilmvideo.com

(For bulk purchases, please contact the publisher.)

10 9 8 7 6 5 4 3 2   020314

Printed in the United States of America

♾ This paper meets the requirements of ANSI/NISO Z39.48-1992 (Permanence of Paper)

This book is dedicated to:

My sons, Julius Pryor IV and Christopher J. Pryor.
Be ready to extend yourself to complete the mission.

Contents

Foreword

Julius Pryor III is an extraordinary storyteller. And his stories always have a point. Stories are the primary medium by which we learn and retain knowledge. Stories are essential when there is something important to learn. We are facing just such a time.

Much has been written about how disruptive technology has changed business, industry, and organizations (iTunes, Amazon, robotic manufacturing, online advertising, social networks, privacy concerns, etc.). Disruption not only affects organizations, it affects each of us as individuals—when is the last time you saw someone use a key to open or lock their car door?

There is an old saying that goes, "things ain't like they used to be." Well, they never were, and they never will be again. Change has always been a part of the human condition. But, we have a natural aversion to change, even small, incremental change. Recently, the pace of change has become mind-boggling. That is why *Thriving in a Disruptive World* is so timely. The book serves as a call to action and a recipe for what action to take.

Julius introduces us to six critical concepts to help us manage through the escalating and accelerating pace of change. He not only lists and defines these precepts; he illustrates them with stories that help us see how to utilize them to be effective in an ever-changing world.

The principles are simple—Clarity, Quantum Thinking, Hyper-Collaboration, Agility, Passion, and Faith. Equip yourself to understand and use his ideas, and you too can be among those who thrive in a disruptive world. Welcome to the journey.

James O. Rodgers, FIMC
The Diversity Coach™
Author of *Managing Differently: Getting 100% from 100% of Your People 100% of the Time*

Preface

> "Sometimes the questions are complicated
> and the answers are simple."
>
> Theodor Geisel (Dr. Seuss)

As you read the following, don't think of it as a conventional book. Rather, think of it as an idea template. I'm going to share six critical concepts to take with you everywhere. This is practical information—to be used, to prepare you, and to help you accomplish your goals.

Today we find ourselves in uncertain times. Many of us are out of work, in transition, or simply trying to figure out our next move. This is a *time of disruption*.

My goal is to provide six concepts to serve you in navigating a *disruptive world*.

As human beings, we grow and develop in reaction to our surroundings: we interact with one another, we relate to our cultures, and we respond to our challenges. As our environments change, so do our behaviors. That said, as we watch uncertainty unfold around us, we are unsettled. We do not feel safe.

As we move deeper into the twenty-first century, the world will continue to become a more disruptive place. We are all going to be challenged further by our surroundings. The objective is not just to survive, but to *thrive*.

Understand that there are huge opportunities in times like these. In fact, difficult times—when we don't feel safe—offer the most potential. Without a comforting sense of safety, we are more willing to seek the potential of uncertain opportunities. We have less to lose and more to gain.

To be successful, we all have to become **more comfortable being uncomfortable**. We have to be confident in the prospects of what we don't yet know. We have to be willing to fail while stretching for an achievement greater than our last.

These six concepts are valuable for thriving in any kind of disruptive environment. They are relevant to business people wanting to succeed in a disruptive economy. They are supportive to college students striving for excellence in a sluggish job market. Teams and organizations looking for a competitive edge on a disruptive global playing field can utilize them. They will also be valuable to single parents burning both ends of the candle and trying to provide for their family.

Use this book in whatever way makes sense for you—tailor the lessons to fit your situation and circumstances—but use it!

Acknowledgments

Thank you to:

My mother and father, Barbara Pryor and Dr. Julius Pryor Jr., MD, DDS, FACS.

My sister and brother, Pam Pryor Grace, MBA and Dr. Jonathan A. Pryor, MD, FACS.

Morehouse College, where I learned to continue to learn.

My Omega Psi Phi Fraternity Brothers and Psi Chapter.

My Line Brothers—My Dad's Nine: A true hyper-collaborative team.

The US Navy, where I learned that you can delegate authority, but not responsibility.

Dr. R. Roosevelt Thomas Jr., Jim Rodgers, Jack Ward, and Sharon D'Agostino.

Jim Ellis, Dean, Marshall School of Business, University of Southern California.

Ray Stanford, Cathy Stanford, and Gene Caudle.

Special thanks to Mary Margaret Murphy for valuable editing input. I appreciate your diligence and encouragement.

Everyone who has helped me on the journey—THANK YOU.

Introduction

"Our greatest glory is not in never falling,
but in rising every time we fall."

Confucius

In the Navy

I was a brand-spanking-new navy officer assigned to my first ship, the USS *Okinawa*. The ship was based in San Diego, but already deployed on a six-month exercise. I had to meet the ship in the Philippines.

This was my first time outside of the United States, and when the plane landed in Manila, I was overwhelmed. I was in sensory overload: the mass of people in the airport, the heat, the humidity, the language, the traffic, and the noise. I didn't know where to go or what to do—I was totally confused.

Fortunately there was a navy lieutenant there to pick up some other sailors who jumped their ship in Australia. The Australian authorities put them on a flight back to the nearest naval base. They did not show up, and he approached me and said, "Ensign, you look totally lost who are you, and where are you going?" I told him I was assigned to the USS *Okinawa* and was trying to figure out how to get there. He replied, "Oh yeah, the *Brokinawa*—she's in Subic Bay with engine problems. They had to tow her most of the way from San Diego. I have a jeep; I'll give you a lift. Come on, rookie."

After a tedious and bumpy three-hour ride, we finally arrived at what was then the largest US naval installation in the Pacific: Naval Station Subic Bay. I was jet-lagged, hungry, and exhausted. I was upside down—in shock—trying to come to grips with a new environment and a new culture.

The ship was indeed undergoing repairs to its engines, but rough weather was headed our way, and all the ships in port had to get underway to avoid being in danger when the storm hit. As soon as we cleared the breakwater, *I was seasick!* That is why after all this time, I still remember the name of that storm: *Typhoon Irma*. My first thought was—*I am an officer in the navy! How am I going to make it if I am seasick, and we are not even in blue water yet?* In fact, we were barely a few yards from the pier—and headed into a typhoon! Within minutes, I leaned over the rail, puked my guts out, and was totally humiliated in front of the commanding officer (CO) and my department head. So much for first impressions— what a great way to begin my life in the navy!

When it happened, although it seems humorous now, I thought it was the end of my career—I did not know how I was ever going to recover, let alone move forward. In fact, when I reported to the bridge the following day, the watch standers had a mop and a bucket with my name on it, just in case I felt ill. I was the butt of all the jokes the rest of the week.

Truth be told, we all go through rough times at various points in our lives. When I got seasick and puked all over myself and the ship, the CO just laughed and said, "Go change your shirt and get ready to stand watch. You have been initiated!"

I had a very experienced and caring chief petty officer (CPO) who took an interest in me and taught me a great deal about how to be a leader. There was a team of officers and enlisted personnel, some good, some bad, some in-between, who helped me. And yes, there were a few assholes, but for the most part, I picked up something valuable from all of them. They taught me how to be confident, to be forceful, to have command presence. My chief took me aside and explained how to relate to the men in my division: even if I did not have the answers, even though I was new, they expected me to know my stuff, because I was their division officer—I was their leader. I picked up critical lessons about attention to detail, focus, and discipline. I also learned that you can delegate authority, but not responsibility. I learned so much in those first few months at sea that continues to serve me well today. I had help all along the way. In fact, that was the most important lesson: That we all need help from time to time, and you can never go wrong by taking time to help someone else.

During my first few months at sea we "crossed the line" (the equator), visited Sydney and Perth, Australia; Hong Kong; Diego Garcia; and Pearl Harbor, Hawaii. I finally got my sea legs, and by the time I reported to my first professional school, SWOS (Surface Warfare Officer School), I was not only a shellback (a designation given to those who cross the equator), but I was salty. In fact, I had more experience on a combat ship at sea than 90 percent of the people in my SWOS class!

By the time we ended our deployment and returned to San Diego, the crew had turned the ship's reputation around. She would never again be called the Brokinawa—we were now the Steamin' Machine!

Hot Wash Up – In the Navy:

1. To be successful, we need help all along the way. Don't be afraid to ask for it!

2. The situation is never as bad as it seems— you can handle it; just keep moving forward.

3. Sometimes you have to puke your guts out to get your sea legs!

Concept 1: Clarity

"Sometimes in order to see the light, you have to risk the dark."

Dr. Iris Hineman, *Minority Report*

C larity of intention, mission, and direction empower us to move forward deliberately and decisively. Yet often, clarifying our goals and setting realistic timelines for them is difficult. Whether we are a part of a large organization, an intimate team, or flying solo, we must be absolutely sure of our purpose and course. We should then work to develop an outcome orientation. Otherwise, we lack objective and become stuck. Clarity predisposes us to being decisive and direct, enables our success, and is foundational to thriving in a time of disruption.

> "The greatest mistake you can make in life is continually fearing that you'll make one."
> Elbert Hubbard

Good Intentions

Jim was a single guy working in the family business. He found out he was going to inherit a huge fortune when his sickly father died, and he decided he needed a wife with whom to share his fortune.

One evening at a meeting, he spotted the most striking woman he had ever seen. Her beauty took his breath away. "I may look like an ordinary man," he said to her, "but in a few months, my father will die, and I'll inherit a large, multimillion dollar inheritance."

Impressed, the woman obtained his business card, and six days later, *she became his stepmother!*

Good intentions can sometimes lead to unintended consequences.

Jim never told the woman what he wanted! If you are not clear about what you want, how can you ever get it?

> **"A great deal of what FedEx has accomplished was built on lessons I learned in the Marine Corps."**
> Fred Smith

The Rule of Three

One of the basic tenets of the Marine Corps is the **rule of three**. Each person in the chain of command has three things to be concerned with.[1] Corporals manage three privates, sergeants manage three corporals, and so on and so forth. Having clarity of mission and direction will help you move forward in a more deliberate manner. The Marines figured this out through trial and error. They realized if they gave a marine two tasks to complete, he got bored and lost focus. With four or more jobs, he was overwhelmed and could not do any of them well. They eventually came up with a doctrine that kept everything manageable—three was the magic number.

Some of you are dealing with too many goals, and too few of them have clear alignment with your personal objectives. If you take on an overabundance of tasks, you will be unable to do them all well. For the most part these things are transactional; they are tactical actions, not strategic in and of themselves. Separate the critical from the trivial and focus on your personal end game.

You can develop a personal process that follows the "rule of three": **Be Clear, Concise, and Confident.**

---

[1] David H. Freedman, "Corps Values," *Inc.*, April 1, 1998.

Using the **rule of three** is another method for gaining clarity. *Say it, write it, visualize it, and dream about it.* Do whatever works for you, but get serious about doing it!

> **"Life is not important except in the impact it has on other lives."**
> Jackie Robinson

Leveraging Diversity

I was a sales manager with a pharmaceutical company. We had a relatively unique product that was a monthly injectable drug used in the palliative treatment of prostate cancer.

As I continued to learn about the market for this drug and also looked at the patient population that was most at risk, I was surprised to learn that the disease disproportionately affects Black men. African American men are nearly 60 percent more likely to develop prostate cancer as compared to Caucasian men and have a mortality rate that is nearly 2.5 times higher (data from NIMHD[2]).

The medical specialty that treats this malady is urology. Less than 4 percent of the board-certified urologists in the USA were African American, yet they were treating a much higher rate of prostate cancer disease in their practices.

Their patients presented with prostate cancer, of all stages, at a higher rate than for physicians in the general

---

[2] "Health Disparities – Prostate Cancer," National Institute on Minority Health and Health Disparities, http://www.nimhd.nih.gov/hdFactSheet_pc.asp

population. I concluded that there were many factors for this, but one of the primary reasons was the demographic makeup of their practices.

I was not able to get specific numbers, as some of my evidence was anecdotal, but I was confident that Black urologists, though relatively small in number, were seeing a disproportionate group of patients with higher rates of prostate cancer.

Immediately I saw this as a business opportunity for the company. We had a product for the palliative treatment of the disease. If we spent a small amount of invested capital and a small amount of invested time with this group of physicians, it would pay a marked dividend to our company in terms of unit sales and market share gains.

Some people in the company were initially reluctant to be fully supportive of my efforts to engage with this group. They had not spent a great deal of time in these communities or with this group of physicians and were skeptical. They were not keen to engage this physician population and did not see the potential return.

There was a default assumption that this was a waste of time and effort. I, on the other hand, was very familiar with these doctors. I saw them as trusted frontline professionals and instinctively realized the potential. I was able to eventually influence the leadership team at the company that this approach made sense and that it could be a huge win in terms of sales and targeted revenue. I pushed forward, was able to get a few prominent leaders in the company to support me, and amazingly, we began to see results: market share increased, revenue was grown exponentially, and top-line growth was greater than ever before.

However, something else came out of this effort that was just as, if not more, important. We were able to develop a long-lasting relationship with this group of physicians. We supported their professional organization, *The Urology Section of the National Medical Association (NMA)*. We were able to do enormous work with education on prostate cancer, and we also developed prostate cancer screening events for an at-risk patient population. We organized and supported a national effort to establish prostate cancer support groups. **We provided a cutting-edge product for treatment and did all of this for an underserved and overlooked group of patients.** .

I was able to drive clarity about outcomes and to influence leadership by delivering lucidity relative to leveraging diversity to directly drive a revenue target!
The result was:

- *increased sales* in the marketplace;
- a unique connection and *recognition of African American urologists*; and
- *valuable prostate cancer education* for an at-risk patient population.

This was an amazing accomplishment in how to **leverage diversity to drive clearly defined outcomes. A successful strategic diversity process should always align with critical organizational objectives.**

I knew I had finally succeeded when everyone in the company wanted to take credit for our success!

> **"People will forget what you said and people will forget what you did, but people will never forget how you made them feel."**
> Maya Angelou

James Bond

When movie producer Cubby Broccoli obtained the rights to the James Bond novels, he instinctively felt that he had stories that would translate into a profitable series of film adventures for the now-famous fictional secret agent. He picked a seasoned director, Terence Young, to do the first film in the series, *Dr. No.*

Picking an actor to play the part of James Bond proved more difficult. He wanted someone who could be an action star and someone who had the look of the character described in the novels. They initially wanted Cary Grant to play the part but could not get him to commit to multiple films. They considered other actors, but for one reason or another, they were not available. They finally decided on Sean Connery, who was a relatively unknown actor at the time. Not everyone was sure he was the best person for the role, and the author of the novels, Ian Fleming, was not happy that this "rough" Scottish actor had been chosen to play Agent 007.

However, once Cubby was clear that this was his "Bond," everyone else got clarity. Terence Young personally took Connery under his wing and proceeded to smooth the "rough edges" so that he became the James Bond we all know today. Terence Young was sophisticated, well-traveled, stylish, and a member of the British upper crust. He taught Connery how to walk, how to turn a phrase, and how to pick the right wine. He took him to his tailor and gave him panache. He gave him confidence and clarity about the character he was portraying as James Bond. He was not only Connery's film director, he was his personal director. Even today, after other actors have played the part, many still consider Sean Connery to be the definitive James Bond. After seeing the finished film, Ian Fleming even came around, altering the fictional Bond's background to reflect Scottish roots!

Once Connery was selected and producer Broccoli made it clear that this was the guy, everything was in place to develop one of the most successful film series in cinema history! If the other producers, the studio, the cast, and the crew had no confidence in this unknown actor, the entire project would have fallen apart. This is why clarity is so important.

Hot Wash Up – Clarity:

1. Be Decisive, Direct, and Genuine

2. Remember: The Rule of Three.

3. Stay Focused: Once you are clear, everything falls into place. Be prepared for the success that follows.

Concept 2:
Quantum Thinking

> "I don't pretend we have all the answers. But the questions are certainly worth thinking about."
>
> Arthur C. Clarke

Q uantum mechanics is the part of physics that tells us how the things that make up atoms work. It is a mathematical construct for much of modern physics and chemistry; it helps us understand and allows us to make sense of the smallest things in nature. Subatomic particles and electromagnetic waves behave in weird ways. "Quantum" is a Latin word that means "how much."

Quantum mechanics defies the rules of the physical world. Particles can occupy two or more places at the same time, and yet quantum physics is the most accurate scientific theory ever tested. Although the sub-atomic world is different from the physical world, the physical world is built on sub-atomic particles.

In 1925, Werner Heisenberg described the Heisenberg Uncertainty Principle, which says that the more we know about where a particle is, the less we can know about how fast it is going and in which direction; in other words, the more we know about the speed and direction of something small, the less we can know about its position. Physicists usually talk about the momentum in such discussions instead of talking about speed. Momentum is just the speed of something in a certain direction multiplied by its mass. The reason behind this uncertainty principle is that we can never know both the location and the momentum of a particle.[3]

Quantum mechanics explains complexity, and to do what I refer to as **quantum thinking**, you have to see what is going on just below the surface. You have to look around corners and bend your perspective.

> **"Discovery consists of seeing what everybody has seen, and thinking what nobody has thought."**
> Albert Szent-Györgyi

The Sexiest Man

Ryan Reynolds was selected as *People Magazine*'s sexiest man of 2011. Why was he chosen over all of the entertainers and celebrities available? To answer the question, you have to remember what project Reynolds was headlining in 2011. He had recently been chosen to play the part of comic book superhero The Green Lantern in a big-budget movie about to be released.

Warner Bros. was the studio producing the film. The Green Lantern is a character from the DC Comics universe. Reynolds was on the cover of both *People Magazine* and

---

[3] Werner Heisenberg, *The Physical Principles of the Quantum Theory* (Mineola, New York: Dover Publications, 1949).

Entertainment Weekly (EW) in successive months. Warner Bros., DC Comics, *People*, and *EW* are all operating units of the Time Warner media conglomerate. So what at first glance seems like a very competitive selection for the "Sexiest Man" was actually savvy marketing. This was not at all a contest to pick the Sexiest Man. This was not a beauty contest. This was a marketing strategy to sell a motion picture product.

If they could have figured out a way to place him on the covers of *Time* and *Sports Illustrated* (also units of Time Warner), he would have been there too. You can rest assured that after the company has squeezed any profit out of DVD sales, we will see the film migrate down the chain to appear on HBO, then TNT and TBS (all units of Time Warner).

Time Warner made a tidy profit—on what was by all accounts not a very good movie—because of their smart marketing campaign!

There is nothing wrong with a company leveraging its assets to sell a product or service, but situations like this one, which is a relatively benign example, play out all of the time. You don't see it unless you are able to do **quantum thinking.** To think in quanta infers going beyond *analytical thinking* with its emphasis on direct facts, data, and observation. You are actually considering how to pull disparate points together to deliver context and meaning. It is a natural expansion of critical thinking, but requires you to have a multi-dimensional perspective.

> **"That's been one of my mantras—focus and simplicity. Simple can be harder than complex: You have to work hard to get your thinking clean to make it simple. But it's worth it in the end because once you get there, you can move mountains."**
> Steve Jobs

Apple vs. the World

Having the ability to touch, feel, and empathize are just as important as being able to see things with a linear methodology. The Apple iPod is a case study. When the iPod was initially released for sale, the Microsoft Zune had been on the market almost three years and had thirty gig of memory. The iPod had only 10 gig of memory, yet was an immediate success! Why? The iPod was unique in how it felt and how it looked. The Zune has been described as "clunky and ugly." The iPod had *cool factor.*

Steve Jobs looked at his work through the eyes of a designer and artist, while Bill Gates' view was that of a computer scientist—an engineer. Their respective company cultures reflect the personalities of their founders. Products from Apple and products from Microsoft are direct reflections of their cultural roots. You produce "cool" products when you do quantum thinking. You design "clunky" functional products when you do analytical thinking. The iPod had sensory appeal beyond functionality, which was lacking in the Zune. It was a complete product. You can see the same attributes in other Apple platforms from computers to smart phones. Even when you compare an Apple Mac to other competing products, you see unique design characteristics. The Apple device appeals to human interface. It feels good, and it looks attractive.

People with an artistic sensibility are best suited to do this— an MFA (Master in Fine Arts) rather than an MBA (Master in Business Administration). I'm not suggesting that having skill sets in traditional management are no longer applicable, but we are now in an era when having a conceptual perspective is increasingly valuable.

> **"Experts often possess more data than judgment."**
> Colin Powell

Analytics

Analytics is the ability to sift through and analyze digital information and other data to make sense of it. Companies like IBM are staking their future on being able to do this better than anyone else. Some say that the attacks of September 11 could have been predicted if we had the ability to pull a number of disparate bits of information together. If we could have somehow gathered all of the relevant data, some analyst could then make conceptual sense of it.

I said earlier that clarity requires being outcome-driven and having defined goals. This positions **quantum thinking** as a force multiplier to drive desired outcomes. When I talk about this unique way of thinking, people in traditional hierarchical organizations usually push back— they are uncomfortable. Even in times of disruption, some leaders are opposed to seeing the future—it is threatening to the people in charge (them).

You want to develop an ability to see the periphery and look around corners. To be able to pull threads together, make sense of them, and see through the clutter is what will give you a competitive advantage. You see what others don't. In a disruptive world, we are being overwhelmed by a tsunami of information: cable TV pundits, radio talkers, blogs, twitter feeds, texts, and all of the other ways that we access "stuff." In order to separate that which is valuable from that which is trivial, you must conceptualize—to see what is actually taking place.

> "As you think, so shall you become."
> Bruce Lee

For Smart People

Olny srmat poelpe can raed tihs.

I cduoln't blveiee taht I cluod aulaclty uesdnatnrd waht I was rdanieg. Thc phaonmneel pweor of the hmuan mnid! Aoccdrnig to rseearch at Cmabrgide Uinervtisy, it deosn't mttaer in waht oredr the ltteers in a wrod are, the olny iprmoatnt tihng is taht the fsirt and lsat ltteer be in the rghit pclae. The rset can be a taotl mses, and you can sitll raed it wouthit a porbelm. Tihs is bcuseae the huamn mnid deos not raed ervey lteter by istlef, but the wrod as a wlohe. Amzanig huh? Yaeh, and I awlyas tghuhot slpeling was ipmorantt!

The above passage shows how powerful and adept the human mind is.

In order to be a quantum thinker, you have to use your entire mind. You have to pull back and zoom in at the same time to see what is actually there. There is always something unique and revealing just beneath the surface. Open your eyes and open your mind. See the whole picture!

> **"The most important thing to remember is this: To be ready at any moment to give up what you are, for what you might become."**
> W. E. B. Du Bois

Default Assumption

The following observations draw on the work of K. C. Cole, science writer for the *Los Angeles Times* and Professor at the Annenberg School of Communications and Journalism at the University of Southern California.

A man is driving his son to a football game, and the car gets stuck on the railroad tracks. A train comes, and the father is killed but the child survives; however, the child is in critical condition. Paramedics get the boy to the hospital, and the surgeon says, "I can't operate on this boy; he's my son."

How is this possible?

Whenever I ask people to answer the question posed by this story, the responses are sublime to ridiculous. It turns out that the surgeon is the boy's mother!

We automatically assume that the surgeon is a man. Why do we think like this? Rather than calling this a stereotype, let's consider the concept of **default assumptions.** A default assumption leads us to jump to conclusions before we have completely considered all of the facts. Much of this behavior is embedded in our deep subconscious.[4]

---

[4] K. C. Cole, "Why does 'CEO' Mean 'White Male'?," *Los Angeles Times*, October 18, 2012.

As we grow and develop as human beings, we are exposed to messages and images and things that we experience. More often than not, we fall back on our defaults, which in most cases are based on anecdotes and personal experience.

It is impossible to have experienced every situation and every permutation and every possibility. Therefore, to get through the day, we rely on our default assumptions.

My *assumption* is that most of the people reading this are intelligent, so why do we continue to make assumptions about other people that are wrong and unfair?

Why do we judge without taking time to look at and to think about situations and circumstances based on facts?

Even when our assumptions are proven wrong, we still hold onto them. So, when we see a *female fighter pilot* or a *Black chairman of the Joint Chiefs of Staff* or a *gay CEO* or a *Hispanic physicist* or an *Asian film director*, we go to the back of our minds, and without even pausing, say that this is an "exception."

Keep in mind that to have default assumptions does not infer that you are a homophobe, a racist, or a sexist. It simply means that you are human. **Well then, why is this important—why does any of this matter?**

This is why: if you are making a decision on hiring someone, or promoting someone, or picking someone for a developmental position; if you are on a jury deciding who is guilty or innocent or who deserves the death penalty; if you are a physician preparing to treat a patient; or if you are in any number of situations where decisions have to be made that could influence someone's life, then it matters a great deal.

The more that you are aware of how you think, the more you are aware of how you make decisions, then the more you are aware of your **personal default assumptions**. Only then, will you be able to actively make adjustments to correct for them.

I'm not asking you change who you are. However, I do want you to have the ability to make adjustments to your behaviors—especially when it is going to deliver a more effective outcome.

Hot Wash Up – Quantum Thinking:

1. Critical thinking gives you facts; conceptual thinking gives you big picture. Quantum thinking combines both and gives a context that reveals what is actually occurring.

2. There is a tsunami of unimportant, trivial stuff being passed off as valuable information— you have to look closely to see what is relevant.

3. We are much more powerful than we give ourselves credit for—stretch your mind!

Concept 3:
Hyper-Collaboration

C onsider the qualities that a successful team possesses. It would be very unusual for one person to possess all the specialized skills to play every position on a professional sports team. Even golf, considered an individual sport, has an unofficial team approach with caddies and swing coaches to lean on for advice. Having people who can augment the skills that you lack allows you to focus on your strengths and to stay targeted on outcomes.

Something else concerning collaboration: it happens naturally. Human beings, as a matter of fact, are social creatures. We want to be around and connected to other people. The most successful organizational models in the twenty-first century will be intrinsically collaborative and symbiotic. Create the right culture to enhance collaboration, build a powerful team, and you will be unstoppable!

> **"Finding good players is easy,
> getting them to play as a team is another story."**
> Casey Stengel

The Navigator

I was in the navy at sea on a Western Pacific exercise, and we were about to refuel with the oiler. An oiler is an auxiliary navy ship that specializes in refueling other ships at sea while underway. This is accomplished while both ships are moving and is one of the most dangerous and complex of naval maneuvers. This particular exercise was made even more difficult because we were in a rainstorm, in rough seas, and it was being done at night.

The navigator had to take the deck because the OOD (officer of the deck) was confused and lost the picture. He was unable to focus and didn't know what orders to give for the safe maneuvering of the ship. We were now on a collision course with the oiler!

The commanding officer relieved the OOD and nodded to the navigator. The entire bridge crew was silent. He calmly stepped forward and took command. He knew what needed to be done; the Captain trusted him, everyone in the crew trusted him, and he trusted himself—he was confident. He forcefully barked out a series of orders to the helm (steering) and lee helm (engines). He communicated with the forward and aft lookouts. He sent a message to the oiler via the signal bridge. He brought the ship around and in a few minutes had us parallel to and alongside the oiler. Soon we were receiving fuel and stores. It was a successful turnabout.

One of the most critical billets on a navy ship is that of the navigator. The navigator plots the course, determines what speed the ship will use, and decides where we make our turns. The navigator also gives input on where to pick up supplies and do refueling. The navigator knows the ship and the crew. He has to understand their capabilities. He has to understand how fast the ship can go, its maneuvering profile, how hard it can turn, and how fast the engines can run.

The navigator has to know how to read a chart. He has to determine where the rocks and shoals are, where the deep water and shallow water is, where the dangerous eddies are, and what the tide patterns will be. He has to understand aides to navigation and shipping patterns. He also has to be aware of weather.

He has to know ports of call: will we be able to tie up alongside a pier or have to anchor out? What are the port capabilities? Is there a local coast guard? Is a harbor pilot available? Is there heavy shipping traffic?

Even after taking all of these things into account, there are inevitably occurrences that knocked us off course: storms, engine casualties, heavy wind, set, and drift.

We are often called on to do a mission in support of a natural disaster or calamity, like a hurricane or earthquake. The navigator has to quickly plot a course to ensure that the ship can safely get to where it needs to be at the time it needs to be there.

Everything he does is accomplished because he has a great team of people supporting the mission. This collaborative approach is critically important to do his job, and it is even more important to be able to complete your mission now.

We all need people to help us navigate life—they are there. You have to recognize them and utilize their skills to get to your next port safely!

In our own lives, we have to understand how to navigate in a number of different circumstances: navigate organizational cultures; navigate our personal lives; navigate in a disruptive economic environment.

You have to remember you are not alone. There are people who can and should act as your personal navigators. You only have to ask them to help. However, before you can get the navigator to help, you need to be clear about where you are going. Once the destination is known, ask your navigator to plot a course and help you get there. Even then, there will be storms and other unexpected occurrences that act to throw you off track. But if your ship is well-constructed and your crew is able, you'll get there.

Don't be afraid to ask the navigator for help in reaching your destination.

> **"Individual commitment to a group effort, that's what makes a team work, a company work, a society work, a civilization work."**
> Vince Lombardi

The Hyper-Collaborative Team

The New England Patriots are one of the most successful franchises in the National Football League—since 1996, they have claimed the AFC East Division Championship twelve times, won the Conference Championship six times, and taken home three Super Bowl trophies. They have more Super Bowl appearances in the last twenty-five years than any other team and have repeatedly broken their own record for most wins in a decade, most recently with 126 wins from 2003 to 2012.

Yet every year, their team roster sports dozens of new players; in fact, sometimes their turnover rate approaches as much as 70 percent. How can a team that has so much player turnover win so consistently? It is because of the **hyper-collaborative culture** that they create and maintain year after year. The Patriots' franchise, perhaps more than any other team in professional sports, breeds an environment for success and is an excellent model to look to as they exemplify so many characteristics of a **hyper-collaborative team.**

The Patriots' organization is always clear about their number one objective—winning championships and, ultimately, Super Bowls. To this end, they place their emphasis on the team's results rather than on the successes of individual players. Frequently this means players and staff must set aside individual differences for the loftier goal of doing what is in the best interest of the team as a whole.

If a starter gets hurt and is no longer able to deliver results, that player is replaced by a back-up without sentiment or damaged egos. In fact, that is how Tom Brady came to be the starting quarterback, stepping up to what would become the role of a lifetime, when Drew Bledsoe suffered an injury in the second game of the 2001 season. They are results-oriented and run their team accordingly.

In addition, the Patriots' proven leadership and stable ownership group have established a foundational support mechanism that allows their organization to function at the very highest level. This strong foundation creates an environment that helps incoming players to quickly find their niche. With this extra support, every team member is able to thrive and make his best contribution to the team's objectives. Even senior players are expected to participate in supporting new talent, ensuring that every team member demonstrates his full potential come game day.

Head coach Bill Belichick, who also serves as the team's general manager, leads the staff. He is known for being an innovative coach who is unafraid of risk. Described as a student of the game, Belichick is extremely focused and detail-oriented. He is always breaking down video and analyzing an opponent's defensive and offensive schemes, looking for every gap in a competitor's game to exploit on the field. Belichick expects the same focus and attention to detail of every member of his team, on and off the field. He entrusts quarterback Tom Brady to set an example for the rest of team—staying focused on team objectives. In spite of being a recognized celebrity beyond his sport, Brady does not allow himself to be distracted by his status, an easy trap that many professional athletes fall prey to.

But it is the Patriots' discipline that—more than any other hyper-collaborative attribute—takes their game to the next level. While every professional sports team is physically rigorous in their training, the Patriots exhibit a level of discipline in their play execution unmatched in the NFL.

By practicing until their communication reaches a level that does not require verbal play calls, they are able to employ a series of no-huddle offensive plays that not only are clutch in a crunch but also leave their opponents scrambling to keep up with a fast-paced game. During seasons when overall team talent is somewhat lacking, it is this discipline—this caliber of training and play execution—that ensures they are always a top contender. Even when they do not win, they remain competitive and in the game to the very end, usually losing by only a few points.

The Patriots may be made up of a group of individuals, but they function more akin to an organism, and *exhibit almost every characteristic of a hyper-collaborative team:*

1. **Focus on details.**
2. **Innovate and take risks.**
3. **Clarity of goals and objectives.**
4. **Communicate clearly and concisely.**
5. **Provide calm and consistent leadership.**
6. **Create a culture that is supportive of success.**
7. **Discipline—constant training, practice, and development.**
8. **Emphasize team results ahead of individual accomplishments.**
9. **Analyze their competition, exploiting competitors' weaknesses.**
10. **Maintain a historical perspective—understand their cultural roots.**

> **"The crème never rises to the top, it is pushed, pulled or placed there."**
> Dr. R. Roosevelt Thomas, Jr.

SEALs vs. Pirates

On April 8, 2009, Somali pirates attacked and boarded the MV *Maersk Alabama* in the Gulf of Aden off Somalia. A merchant ship bound for Mombasa, Kenya, the *Alabama* was carrying 17,000 metric tons of cargo and a crew of 20. Having received anti-piracy training, the crew was prepared to engage in anti-piracy tactics. They successfully prevented the pirates from taking command of the ship by rerouting engine and steering controls away from the bridge. Unable to navigate the ship and its valuable cargo back to their base in Somalia, the pirates instead took Captain Richard Phillips hostage, escaping in one of the ship's lifeboats.

This was the first pirate seizure of an American-flagged ship since the nineteenth century. With piracy in the region having become an increasing problem, a multinational **anti-piracy task force** had been put into place a few months earlier. The role of this task force was to actively deter, disrupt, and suppress piracy threats.

The pirates expected to be offered a ransom for Captain Phillips—this was the usual playbook. It had become customary for owners of hijacked merchant ships and oil tankers to pay a ransom in order to expedite the release of their ships and cargo. However, the response the pirates received was not what they expected.

Since this was an American-flagged vessel and there was an American navy officer in command of the anti-piracy task force, the US was determined to set a precedent for a swift outcome. The US Navy was called in to what had become a hostage rescue operation, and within hours, three navy ships were on the scene.

The Combined Maritime Forces operation is a 27-nation effort. **US Navy Rear Admiral Michelle Howard** had assumed command of the anti-piracy task force (Expeditionary Strike Group 2) just three days earlier on April 5. Michelle Howard was not new to "firsts," having already blazed a trail for women in the US military: she was the **first Black woman** to command a combat ship in the US Navy when she was selected as the commanding officer of the USS *Rushmore* (LSD 47) in 1999.

She was the **first woman** to graduate from the US Naval Academy to achieve flag rank, when she was selected for the one-star rank of rear admiral (lower half) in 2007. She was the first Black woman to command an expeditionary strike group as commander of the anti-piracy task force in 2009. She has since been **promoted to the rank of vice admiral** in 2012, becoming the first Black woman to reach the rank of three-star admiral in the US armed forces.

Admiral Howard had to make a number of critical decisions to ensure the operation was successful, and she quickly devised a plan using ships, aircraft, and a large team of military personnel. After an FBI team was unsuccessful in an attempt to negotiate the release of Captain Phillips, a request was made to send in a Navy SEAL team to assist with Phillips' rescue.

After several days, the lifeboat carrying Phillips and the pirates had run out of fuel and food. The USS *Bainbridge* (DDG 96) offered to take the lifeboat under tow to Somalia, and the pirates accepted. Over the night of April 11, the Bainbridge drew the lifeboat closer, bringing the pirates into range of the SEAL team positioned on the fantail. Ready to use deadly force if the orders were given, the Navy was in tactical control.

Increasing winds and rough seas were causing the lifeboat to thrash about, and the pirates were becoming visibly more agitated. With the pirates no longer in control and with Phillips' life as their only remaining bargaining power, navy commanders feared that the captain's life was at stake. Phillips was in imminent danger—a requirement for orders to be given to take the pirates out. With simultaneous shots, Navy SEAL snipers killed the three pirates, and Captain Phillips was safely rescued.

Although aspects of this mission are still classified, it is commonly accepted that SEAL Team Six was responsible for the rescue as the strategy and tactics are hallmarks of their parameters. The mission demonstrated the unique skill sets that are found in SEAL teams, quintessential characteristics of a hyper-collaborative team: clarity, calm leadership, clear and concise communications, innovation, and calculated risk taking.

With the entire operation dependent on a larger team, SEAL Team Six was able to perform their job efficiently, delivering deadly force with accuracy and precision together with the safe rescue of an American citizen—as per their training.

The circumstances of the hostage situation required extraordinary cooperation and teamwork. It also required an organization supportive of the success of its people—the navy demonstrated remarkable ability.

A large part of the mission's success was due to the leadership of Admiral Michelle Howard, who some perceive to be an unlikely hero. Having taken command of the anti-piracy task force as part of a normal command rotation, just three days before Richard Phillips was taken hostage, she did not fit the stereotypical image of a warrior. How did she get to this position, and what is it about the navy's culture that supported her success?

Of course she had to deliver results at every step in her career. From the time she was a mid-shipman at the Naval Academy, she was meeting objectives, and over the years, she rose through the ranks. She served as a division officer, department head, chief engineer, executive officer, and commanding officer, delivering superior results at each command level. She was determined, disciplined, capable, and confident. She is a leader with command presence.

Many organizations send a signal to their people that it is up to them to get mentors; it is up to them to get development. We say that you have to take the initiative for your success. All too often we take our people (who we always say are our most valuable asset), **throw them into the deep end of the pool, and say, *"Now learn how to swim!"***

For Howard to make the effective mission-critical decisions she did during this operation meant that she had to have mastered the operating parameters of the ships she placed on station, special warfare operations, command structure, and officers and crew. She had to have an instinctive feel for who would be best in unit leadership roles; understand how to communicate up and down the chain of command; be effective and calm; lead and then get out of the way to allow her on-scene commanders to do their jobs, all the while maintaining situational awareness of the operation.

However, if we only consider her performance and her singular goal accomplishment, we miss a critical piece of what enabled her promotion to vice admiral and her development as a seasoned leader. As an organization, the Navy is clear about what is required at each level, providing transparency about what it takes to get promoted. From seaman recruit all the way to commanding officer, an entire career path is laid out with organizational mentorship provided every step of the way. In other words, the navy nurtures its personnel. *They not only wanted Howard to succeed, they expected her to succeed!*

The anti-piracy task force was not an administrative function or a shore-duty tour. This was a critical command where lives were on the line and people could be—and indeed were—killed. Vice Admiral Michelle Howard delivered a superb performance within the context of her team, the desired outcome of a requirements-driven organization that wants to see its people do well.

Unlike corporations that can hire senior officers externally, admirals cannot be hired. Rather, they have to be grown within the organization from the ranks of junior officers, mentored, nurtured, and readied for their future successes as leaders.

Top performing teams, the best and most effective organizations, actually mean it when they say that people are their most valuable asset!

> ## "Everything is practice."
> Pele

Extending Yourself to Complete the Mission:

A few more words about Navy SEALs

The Navy SEALs always operate as a high-performance team. Understanding how they accomplish their goals can teach you how to deliver consistently superior results. The SEALs are disciplined, focused, and always clear about objectives. They are outcomes-driven and ready to **extend themselves** to meet all contingencies.

As a navy officer, I had the opportunity to work with and support SEAL teams on various naval exercises and training evolutions. I had a chance to see how they did their jobs and to understand what they refer to as: **"Extending Yourself to Complete the Mission."**

3 Key Concepts:

Clarity of Objectives:
How they strategically communicate objectives is just as important as tactical execution. To speak to a diverse audience requires skills in managing diversity. Members of SEAL teams come from disparate and diverse backgrounds. Yet they have to learn to trust each other. This level of trust is intrinsic; it comes from training together and understanding that everyone on the team has to

meet the same requirements. Everyone is capable, but they are most effective as a team. They always function for the betterment of the team. The team is above all else what matters most. There is humility in what they do. They are not a "swagger" organization—in fact they believe that swagger and macho will deliver bad results. They are very clear about goals and objectives: how do we get in, how do we get out, what are contingency plans, and what are contingencies to the contingency plan. How can they minimize lives lost—how can they use the least lethal force to get the efficacy desired. In other words, they are professionals.

Benefits of a Requirements-Driven Culture:
Organizations that are requirements-driven don't rely on cronyism and personal preferences. A requirements-driven culture leans toward competence and ability. It also indicates that they believe in training—realistic training. When they are not on a mission, they are training. Most of us spend a great deal of our time doing administrative work and wasting time in meetings. We may actually spend 30 percent of our time doing productive work, if that! The NAVSPECWAR (Naval Special Warfare) Command made a decision early on to create a separate administrative support staff, so that the teams could focus 90 percent of their time on training. That is a hallmark of a requirements-driven business model. It is completely focused on delivering desired outcomes. It also infers that in addition to individual competencies, the entire organization is supportive of their success. The larger team of other branches of the military and allies, the DOD (Department of Defense) at large, the JSOC (Joint Special Operations Command), and civilian agencies are there to lend a hand. They are being nurtured and sponsored to succeed in their mission at every level.

Leveraging Global Human Capital—
Passionate Teams Always Win:

To successfully leverage a global team requires trust. To win with a global team infers being able to lead from the middle or the side, not only from the front. SEAL team decision-making is pushed down to lowest level appropriate; at anytime, any member of the team may be called upon to step up to make critical calls. To drive results, future leaders have to be able to inspire and have a passionate vision; they have to get out of the way. The goal is to deliver tangible, clearly defined results. SEALs are trained for physical factors: to be in top physical condition; to have cardiovascular endurance. They are trained to overcome environmental factors: cold, heat, sand, rain, snow, and to function effectively when tired and hungry. The psychological factors are most difficult to work through: mental toughness—the esprit de corps that comes from knowing everyone is capable, focused, and disciplined. Everyone is there for the mission. Navy SEALS are a twenty-first century hyper-collaborative team. They utilize foundational principles of diversity and inclusion to extend themselves to complete the mission.

Hot Wash Up – Hyper-Collaboration:

1. As an individual, be good at what you do, but understand that success is not singular.

2. It is the responsibility of the organization to create a culture that drives and supports success.

3. The best teams are hyper-collaborative and function like organisms.

Concept 4:
Quantum Thinking

> "I am the greatest; I said that even
> before I knew I was!"
>
> Muhammad Ali

A gility is the ability to move quickly and easily and is a core attribute for success in a disruptive world. Musicians Ron and Ernie Isley, of The Isley Brothers, have had hit records in each decade since the early fifties—an amazing accomplishment! When asked what is required to have such longevity, they explained that being able to adapt to current music trends keeps them fresh. Their values have not changed, and they are still making very good music. Agility enables one to revamp and reanimate.

> **"It is not the most intelligent nor strongest of species that survives, but the one most adaptable to change."**
> Charles Darwin

The 70 Percent Solution

As a navy officer, I worked very closely with the Marine Corps. The smallest of the US military services, they are an expeditionary force with a unique approach, perspective, and set of operating principles. Preparing for action on very short lead times, they employ something they call **the 70 percent solution**. They say that if they have 70 percent of their assets, 70 percent of their resources, 70 percent of their supplies, and understand 70 percent of the mission, they are ready to move forward, knowing that they will pick up everything else along the way. "If we wait until we have 100 percent, the mission will be over before we get there."

This forward-leaning, forward-deployed strategy allows them to meet any number of contingencies in the field and exemplifies their maxim that they will "**improvise, adapt, and overcome.**" Most recently, in the war in Iraq, marines took advantage of the facility of social networks to communicate about improvised explosive device (IED) threats. Rather than waiting for traditional review lessons that come months after a conflict at a war college or in a seminar, they created blogs and posted on Facebook and Twitter to relay real-time information up and down the chain of command.

Unlike management protocols of traditional hierarchical organizations that are resistant to informal, low-level communication, the Marine Corps built **elasticity of**

command into their organizational structure, creating a culture for agility. In an ever-changing landscape, they understand that any member of a team may have to step up to meet unpredictable challenges, and they ready themselves accordingly.

> **"Even if you're on the right track,**
> **you'll get run over if you just sit there."**
>
> Will Rogers

Missed Opportunity

When asked to invest in a new form of communication (the telephone), telegraph executives at Western Union responded that the early telephone was a passing fad that had no value. They did not believe the general public would have any interest in talking into this *contraption* when they could simply send a telegram. This is akin to someone at Google saying that the Internet is just a fad. How many of us communicate via telegram today? The telegraph executives were playing to conventional wisdom based on what they were comfortable with. ***They missed a huge opportunity!***

Xerox executives failed to comprehend the potential of some of the pioneering research being conducted at their own Palo Alto Research Center (PARC). They had tunnel vision based on the fact that their business at the time was copy machines and did not fully capitalize on the work that was being done on computers. PARC developed many modern computing technologies such as the graphical user interface (GUI), laser printing, and the Ethernet. In fact, some consider Xerox to have invented the first personal computer, The Xerox Alto. Even though they installed them in Xerox offices worldwide, the Alto was never commercially sold, as they were blind to its sales potential.

Bill Gates and Steve Jobs were inspired by many of their ideas and utilized them to form the basis of modern personal computing. Jobs is quoted as saying, "They just had no idea what they had."[5] In 1980, Jobs invited several key PARC researchers to join Apple so that they could fully develop and implement their ideas. Xerox's business today is very different—no longer just copy machines. They are a technology, document management, and consulting company. However, at the time, *they missed a huge opportunity!*

Kodak was a very innovative company. They not only made photography accessible to everyone, but they also made modern X-rays a routine diagnostic tool. When they invented digital photography in 1975, an internal battle erupted within the company. The executive team complained that the R&D people were driving down profits by wasting time on things like pictures on a TV screen (digital photography). Every smart phone in use today has the ability to take digital photos using technology patented by Kodak. Digital photography has displaced their traditional film business model, and they recently filed for bankruptcy protection. *They missed a huge opportunity!*

---

[5] L. Gordon Crovitz, "Who Really Invented the Internet?," *The Wall Street Journal*, July 22, 2012.

> **"As to the future,
> your task is not to foresee,
> but to enable it."**
> Antoine de Saint-Exupery

Leveraging Opportunity

Many times innovation is serendipitous. Take the case of Viagra (sildenafil). Pfizer scientists were working on a drug to manage hypertension and kept noticing an interesting side effect—all of the test subjects had erections! Viagra became the go-to product for a new category of erectile dysfunction (ED) drugs, creating a multibillion-dollar market for these pharmaceutical products. If the researchers were not agile, they would have simply said, "We have concluded that the drug is not effective for controlling high blood pressure, so our clinical trial is a failure."

Just suppose that they had ignored what the side effect opportunity of this drug was. They would have missed what became one of the biggest-selling pharmaceutical products in Pfizer's history, and many people who suffer from ED would not have been able to benefit from this new therapy. Agility enables you to be astute enough to see unique opportunities when others do not and to quickly take advantage of those opportunities when they do come along.

At some point, being agile infers that you ignore the so-called experts, go with your gut, and move forward. You have to take risks—in fact, in a disruptive world, you have no choice. You either move forward or you die. It's scary and it's unsettling, but if you want to taste the fruit, you have to go out on a limb.

> **"Do the difficult things while they are easy and do the great things while they are small. A journey of a thousand miles begins with a single step."**
>
> Lao Tzu

Staying Relevant

In the late '90s, Netflix entered the movie rental marketplace with a bang, offering flat-rate DVDs by mail with the ultimate goal of expanding their services to Internet streaming media—for which the company is named. Netflix's business model quickly superseded Blockbuster, who has since been in survival mode, suffering from a downward spiral of catch-up in the effort to remain relevant in the at-home movie-viewing industry. Netflix's viral success in the industry also pushed other competitors (Redbox, Hollywood Video) to revisit their service offerings. Netflix has—without a doubt—set the industry standard.

Hyperaware of the fickle nature of his industry's target customers, Netflix cofounder and CEO, Reed Hastings, has become known for his aggressive *agility*—an attribute that has been cause for both his company's wild success and upsetting its loyal customer base. In 2011, Hastings announced he would be splitting Netflix's service offerings into two separate companies requiring separate subscriptions: Internet-streaming media would remain under the Netflix label, while DVD-by-mail services would move under a newly-created label called Qwikster.

Drawing immediate and widespread criticism, Hastings quickly realized that, in his effort to remain ever agile, he had gotten ahead of himself. Recognizing this move was alienating customers in much the same way that Block-buster's late fees had alienated him in the '90s—which had inspired him to start Netflix in the first place—Hastings cancelled the planned Qwikster service less than one month after announcing it. Hastings has forthrightly admitted that his plans for Qwikster were missteps and "not his finest hour."

Yet, the Netflix business platform is still viable and growing. Hastings is continuing to look forward, exploring new ways to further develop Netflix's service offerings to ensure its business model stays relevant. With increased competition from other video-streaming services such as Hulu, YouTube, and Amazon, Netflix is currently looking to expand its services with distinctive original programming.

Netflix programming is expected to draw viewers away from expensive premium cable channels. Consumers are using more diverse points of access for content. Not only TV screens, but laptops, iPads, and handheld screens. In October of 2013, Netflix surpassed HBO in total subscribers due in part to developing original and creative program-ming only available on its digital platform.

Reed Hastings has demonstrated a number of the core attributes of agility, leaving us three very important lessons to be learned: *one*, that in a disruptive world, it is crucial to continually push the envelope in order to thrive; *two*, that in doing so, occasionally you will misstep, evidence that you are taking appropriate risks; and *three*, you cannot be sentimental and fall in love with one business model or one approach, rather you must always be generating new ideas to stay relevant.

When plans fall apart, you must not be disheartened; rather, keep moving forward, remembering the lessons of your missteps and applying them to your future endeavors.

The windshield of a car is much larger than the rearview mirror: what is ahead is more important than what is behind.

"I have a burning desire to be the best."
Marcus Allen

Falling Forward

Even the most capable and accomplished of us have room for improvement. Take former NFL running back and Hall-of-Famer Marcus Allen. A Heisman Trophy winner at The University of Southern California, Allen blasted into the NFL as 1982 Rookie of the Year. In just his second pro season, he led the Raiders to the Super Bowl XVIII title and captured the Super Bowl MVP award. By anyone's measure, he was a top-performing star.

But he wanted more from himself: *"I have a burning desire to be the best."* In the 1985 off-season, Allen began Tae Kwon Do training. Rather than bask in his early successes, he recognized that he was not yet at the top of his game. When asked why he was doing this, he said, "I'm more flexible than ever. I'm stronger without lifting weights, recover more quickly in the huddle, and I've learned to relax my muscles when I'm trapped on the field. That has saved my legs many times." As he continued his career as an NFL superstar, every time he was tackled, he always managed to fall forward. This allowed him to pick up another two or three yards.

In one game he was tackled just short of the goal line and managed to make a critical last move. The newspaper headline the next day showed a picture of him stretched out with a defensive back wrapped around his legs; it read, "Marcus Allen has head, shoulders, and football across the goal line as Raiders Win!"

So even if you are tackled and fall flat on your face, as long as you fall forward, you are making progress!

The additional training gave him even more of an edge in a measureable way: the 1985 season brought him awards for not only NFL MVP, but also Offensive Player of the Year. Marcus Allen is the very definition of agility.

Hot Wash Up – Agility:

1. Agility: Able to move quickly and easily. Agility enables you to revamp and reanimate.

2. The 70 percent solution: Prepare, train, and be ready to make adjustments as you're going down the road.

3. Leverage Serendipity: you never know where the next great idea will be birthed. Be ready for the opportunity that invariably appears. Be persistent, stay connected, and stay engaged.

Concept 5: Passion

Passion: An intense desire or
enthusiasm for something

"Rest in reason; move in passion."
Khalil Gibran

The Passionate Voter

I have been reflecting on the 2012 US presidential campaign. I was trying to understand on a foundational level why it is we are attracted to this or that candidate. It seems that we vote for someone not because of point papers or a particular stand on issues. We vote for people because of an emotional connection to them.

Sarah Palin's acolytes never cared very much about her educational background or accomplishments. They weren't even put off when she resigned as governor of Alaska before her term was completed. They were connected to her on an emotional level—they were passionate about Sarah Palin.

You can say the same about any political candidate that runs for office—especially a national office. You connect on an emotional level to the candidate. That is why Mitt Romney had so much difficulty gaining traction in his quest for the White House. He came off as a two-dimensional character. He was like cardboard. He did not connect on an emotional level with his desired constituents. This was not at all reflective of his résumé or abilities, real or imagined. It was all about how we felt and all about our emotional connection.

This also applies to President Obama. His most ardent supporters connect to him on an emotional level. They desire for him to be "the man." They are enthusiastic about him as a person—his policies and accomplishments notwithstanding. The candidate who runs for national political office has a background and accomplishments, but when making a final decision, we go for the person that moves us on a visceral level.

How can you bring passion to what it is you are pursuing? You have to believe in it. People in leadership roles do not necessarily have to be engaging, but you remember the charismatic ones. You remember people who connected on a deep emotional level and who can get you motivated to the point that you are willing to go above and beyond.

> **"It's not the size of the dog in the fight;**
> **it's the size of the fight in the dog."**
> Mark Twain

Spike Lee's Passion

Director/writer/producer Spike Lee and I were classmates at Morehouse College. Spike was a popular student at Morehouse. He was larger than life, outgoing, and a natural connector. He was a huge sports fan and a raconteur. He was well on his way to becoming his own brand. *I don't think Spike gets the credit he deserves.*

Regardless of the artistic merit or commercial appeal of his films, he does not get the same kind of support for his movies—from the studio system—as other artists. He does not get large marketing budgets and other kinds of financing deals from Hollywood, even though he has delivered great films time and time again.

We are usually presented with the glamorous side of the entertainment industry, but it is a tough business, populated by some slippery and unethical characters. It is a major accomplishment to get one film produced and distributed. Spike has produced a body of work that is entertaining and substantive. His films and documentaries provoke insight that sometimes makes us uncomfortable, but that is the point—to make us think.

He has been a role model and a groundbreaker for many other directors and writers. He has discovered talent and started the careers of numerous people in front of and behind the camera. There is something that I think people miss about Spike because of his colorful personality. In addition to being a graduate of Morehouse College, he is an extremely skilled and proficient film director and writer, who has a Master of Fine Arts from New York University (NYU Tisch School of the Arts), one of the most competitive and prestigious graduate film directing programs in the world. In fact, he is on the teaching faculty at the NYU Tisch School, not as a celebrity or figurehead, but as a full-time professor.

I would say that he has more technical expertise than many of his peers.

What most people don't see about Spike is that he is *passionate* about his work.

He is so passionate about his film projects that he is always taking risks to get them completed, in some cases even placing his own money on the line to bring his work to fruition. As much as he strives to be tactful and diplomatic, his intensity and genius always comes bursting through! He is a *passionate* artist and business-man thriving in a disruptive world. I think, more than anything, love and passion for his art is what drives him forward.

> **"I am learning all the time.
> The tombstone will be my diploma."**
> Eartha Kitt

The Passionate Educator

You know a person is emotionally connected to their work when they are not paid very much and yet come out of their own pocket to purchase supplies. Schoolteachers do this all the time. I am a mentor in the local school system, and I have had the privilege of meeting and working with many great teachers and other leaders in the schools.

For the outstanding work that they do every day and the support they provide for the children in their charge, they exhibit great passion. Every moment that they are "teaching," they exhibit an ability to go above and beyond to support, nurture, and engage the students in their classrooms. We are all fortunate to have such caring and passionate educators in our school systems.

Teachers are under enormous pressure and are constantly being derided and criticized—primarily by the chattering class—yet they show up every day to do their jobs. They believe in what they are doing. They are engaged in a *purpose-driven* profession. They are making a difference for many students who in some cases get no encouragement in their lives other than from a caring and supportive teacher.

I personally can think of a number of great and supportive teachers that I have had over the years that made a difference for me. They encouraged me and pushed me when I needed it. They helped me build confidence in my ability to move forward and accomplish goals in my life. I'll say it again—we are all indeed blessed to have teachers who are passionate about their jobs.

> **"I am standing by him," Pee Wee Reese said to the world. "This man is my teammate."**

Jackie Robinson and Pee Wee Reese: The Passion to be Genuine

"Thinking about the things that happened, I don't know any other ball player who could have done what he did. To be able to hit with everybody yelling at him. He had to block all that out, block out everything but this ball that is coming in at a hundred miles an hour and he's got a split second to make up his mind if it's in or out or down or coming at his head, a split second to swing. To do what he did has got to be the most tremendous thing I've ever seen in sports."

The Boys of Summer, Roger Kahn – 1970

I recently watched the movie *42*, the story of Jackie Robinson's first year in the major leagues. The film tells the story of how Robinson broke the color line in what was then the most important sport in America: Major League Baseball.

Jackie Robinson is by any measure a true American Hero, but what I found interesting was how the film depicted the influence that Jackie Robinson had on the people around him.

Harold Henry "Pee Wee" Reese was the shortstop and captain of the Brooklyn Dodgers in the 1940s and 1950s. He was raised in segregated Louisville, Kentucky. He is quoted as saying that the first time he ever shook a Black man's hand was when he met Jackie Robinson.

The Dodgers were due to play in Cincinnati, and the racial animosity was high. Cincinnati is close to Kentucky, and Reese had many friends and relatives who told him that there would be trouble if Robinson came to play with the Dodgers that week.

When the team took the field to warm up, the boos and racial slurs were thick. Jackie Robinson walked onto the field. Pee Wee Reese walked out to where he was standing and put his arm around him. This gesture would forever mark Reese as a beloved figure in the Black community.

In the film, when asked why he was doing this, Reese replied, "Those are my people up there [booing] and they need to see who I am."

At the dedication of the statue to commemorate the event in 2005, Robinson's widow, Rachel Robinson, said, "It's a historic symbol of a wonderful legacy of friendship, of teamwork, of courage—of a lot of things we hope we will be able to pass on to young people. And we hope they will be motivated by it, be inspired by it, and think about what it would be like to stand up, dare to challenge the status quo, and find a friend there who will come over and support you."

Pee Wee Reese wanted to win the pennant, and he knew Jackie Robinson could help the Dodgers win games. Reese was a man of his time, and there is some debate as to when and where the event actually occurred. However, when people who knew him describe Pee Wee Reese, they say he was a man of courage, character, and humility, never wanting to take credit for what he did to help Jackie Robinson. He was a man of passion.

He was the genuine article—what you see is what you get. He wanted to be on the right side of history. To do that you have to be genuine, you have to be true, and you have to have a passion for what you stand for.

Hot Wash Up – Passion:

1. Channel your emotional energy—the passion of your soul.

2. You know who you are; stop hiding it—be yourself!

3. Follow you instincts and trust your gut. Usually it's right!

Concept 6: Faith

"Faith is taking the first step even when
you don't see the whole staircase."

Dr. Martin Luther King Jr.

MLK

D r. Martin Luther King Jr. was beginning his career as a pastor in the early days of the civil rights movement. He had just been asked to lead the now-historic bus boycott in Montgomery, Alabama, and he was a reluctant leader. He was a well-educated and erudite person who up until that time had viewed his faith from the perspective of an academic and a seminarian.

Now, as he was being asked to step up into a leadership position with the Montgomery Bus Boycott, he had to begin to look at everything with new eyes. His house had recently been fire-bombed, and for the first time *"faith"* was no longer an academic exercise. He had to ask himself if he actually believed that the Lord would look over him and his family. He had to ask himself if his faith was real or just another "fastidious" sermon that he preached enthusiastically from the pulpit.

Martin Luther King's faith was amplified. He believed more strongly than ever that he was being called to do this work for a larger purpose. His faith was reinforced! His faith made him more determined than ever, and **he changed the world** for the better. That can only be said of a few figures in history! Decades after his physical body is gone, Martin Luther King Jr. made a difference for all of us that continues to reverberate well into contemporary times.

Most of us talk a very good game when it comes to faith and our beliefs. But usually, only when faced with difficult circumstances do we get on our knees and ask for salvation. **You have to believe.**

This is no longer something that you **talk about**; now is the time to take action and **do about**. In fact, you can no longer just stick your toe in the water. This is **Baptism by immersion!**

"Do you wish to rise? Begin by descending. You plan a tower that will pierce the clouds? Lay first the foundation of humility."
St. Augustine

"You can never go wrong by helping someone."
Julius Pryor III

Perspective

I was driving towards home. I have a six-year-old truck, and I was lamenting about the condition it was in. I was upset that I didn't have enough money at the time to get the dents repaired. There were blemishes on the uphol-stery where my sons had spilled food. The suspension was squeaking, and it needed a paint job to get the scratches fixed. I needed to get some new tires.

As I continued to drive down the road, I saw a guy on foot with three large grocery bags. It was a very hot day, and he was struggling to carry his load down the road. I stopped and asked if I could give him a lift since I was going in his direction. He said he would appreciate it.

As soon as he placed his groceries in the back seat and sat down in the front passenger seat, he said, "Man, this is a nice truck!" All I could do was laugh. I suppose if you are on foot walking in the hot sun then I did have a very nice truck indeed!

Sometimes we don't realize how fortunate we are. Sometimes we don't know how much we have. We can all do a better job of keeping things in perspective.

If your faith is strong, it will sustain you.

The Guardian Angel

As I was beginning to work on more speaking and consulting projects, there were times when I doubted whether I was good enough, whether or not I could ever be successful.

I had just come from a meeting and was riding the Atlanta train transit system southbound. I took a seat in the forward car, which was not very crowded. In fact there were only two other people in the car, and they were getting off. As I sat down, another person, a woman, entered the car. She was dressed in flight attendant garb. Even though the car was empty, she made a point to sit right next to me.

A meeting I had just left, with a prospective business client, had not gone well.

I was in a down mood, which is unusual for me. I am normally excited about speaking to and meeting other people, but today, I was just feeling low. I pulled out a newspaper and began to read, not even taking time to make small talk with the lady who was sitting right next to me. Usually I will readily speak to people, but I was down in the dumps this time and chose not to say anything.

She immediately struck up a conversation. She said, "I can pick out the business people when I am flying. They are always so serious and like to read. They are always so focused." She then asked, "So, what business are you in?" This was a tough question for me to answer. There were years when I could have answered by saying that I am the vice president of this corporation or I am leading a strategic plan at this company. I've worked in very well-known corporations and have held seemingly important positions. But not that day—this time I said, "I am a speaker, strategist, and provocateur." The irony is that I am a great public speaker, but I said it without any passion. I said it almost in an apologetic way. I was embarrassed that I was calling myself a speaker and provocateur but was not very confident in my abilities.

She persisted. "That sounds exciting; what do you speak about?" I went on to tell her that I talked about becoming more comfortable being uncomfortable. That I told stories about my life and how there were lessons in these various experiences of mine. That I was writing a book about navigating the disruptive world we are all living in. "Oh, that sounds exciting. Tell me more!" I told her even if you fall flat on your face, as long as you fall forward, you are making progress. She laughed. "You are very good at this. You have found your calling; pursue it with gusto!" She then said, "Push forward and follow your passion—keep your faith, it will see you through."

I asked for her e-mail address. She scribbled something on a scrap of paper. I asked her where she would be going today. She just replied, "I love to fly!"

We arrived at my stop. I got off the train, and as I looked back, I could see absolutely no one in that car. As it pulled out of the station, I could not see her or anyone in that first car of the train! I looked at the paper she gave me and saw that it read simply, "Angelica." I looked at the paper again and I smiled.

We all have guardian angels. They are looking after us. They are there to catch us when we fall and lift us up when we are feeling down. They are there to encourage us to pursue our destinies, and they encourage us to fall forward. When we are afraid, they are there—have faith.

We all need help to move forward. And we all have angels to watch over us.

"**The dogmas of the quiet past are inadequate to the stormy present. The occasion is piled high with difficulty, and we must rise—with the occasion. As our case is new, so we must think anew, and act anew.**"
Abraham Lincoln

Being Tested

There are moments in our lives that are there for us to take stock and reflect on where we have been and who we are. These inflection points allow us to take stock of what is important and to remain steadfast. These moments prepare us to meet the challenges that lay ahead and to be ready. Having a *strong faith* is important: it will keep you resolute.

Hot Wash Up – Faith:

1. If your faith is strong, it will sustain you—be resolute.

2. Keep your destination in mind and create a perspective that works.

3. We all need help—and we all have help.

Conclusion

"In times of disruption, there are huge opportunities."

Julius Pryor III

Kinetic Action

It is difficult to get out in front and to lead. When you are following your gut, most people will think you are wrong. Yet you have to move forward. If you are doing what everyone else is doing, if you are following the conventional wisdom, if you stay safe, if you stay in your lane, you may not be following your path.

When Steve Jobs launched the iPad, most critics said it was just a big iPhone.

Even after all of his triumphs with the other Apple products, the conventional wisdom, the naysayers, said he was crazy and that he was wrong this time.

Once again, the critics were wrong, and it was a big hit, leading the way for a new category of tablet computing devices. Apple is now one of the most successful companies in the world.

> ## "You can go your own way!"
> Lindsey Buckingham, Fleetwood Mac

At Amazon.com, some new ideas look like money-losing distractions. The stock market usually reacts negatively to innovation. Amazon CEO Jeff Bezos feels that if new initiatives make strategic sense, a five-to-seven-year payoff is okay: *"We are willing to be misunderstood for long periods of time."*

We are all individuals, and what works for me could be very different from what works for you. So, as we go through life, remember that your flow is a very personal transaction; you decide what it looks like, because only you know what works and what feels right. No one knows *you* better than *you*.

Keep this idea of "flow" in mind at all times. Stop trying to make sense of your life by looking at someone else. Focus on *what makes sense for you*.

> ## "Damn the torpedoes, full speed ahead!"
> Admiral David Farragut

> ## "A flying machine might be evolved by the combined and continuous efforts of mathematicians in one million to ten million years…"
> *New York Times*, October 9, 1903

> **"...We started assembly today..."**
> *The Diary of Orville Wright,* October 9, 1903

Some people are action-oriented and others wait for the proverbial "right moment" to get started. Think about that article from the 1903 *New York Times.* The noted scientists of the day said that in their most expert opinion that it is beyond the scope of man's ability and knowledge to build an airplane. The Wright brothers just went ahead and did it! They ignored the experts. If it's never been done before, what do the "experts" know?

There is never a perfect time to make a bold move, there is never a good time to leave the current situation, there is never going to be a set of ideal circumstances to strike out. It is difficult because we all fear the unknown.

You have to take a leap of faith!

> **"Not everything that counts can be counted, and not everything that can be counted counts."**
> Albert Einstein

The Sextant

As a junior officer in the navy, I had to learn how to fix our position with a sextant as part of my training as a surface warfare officer. All of the junior officers on the ship complained about why we had to learn to use a sextant in an age of satellite navigation and other high tech instrumentation.

Only later did I realize why this was important. The sextant was to remind us of three things:

- At one time, when the ships were made of wood and the men were made of steel, this was the only way to accurately determine your location. You had to be able to fix your position using the stars and the sun.

- This kept us close to our historical roots as officers in the naval service and reminded us of how difficult and dangerous sea travel was in an earlier era.

- If you don't know where you are, you don't know how far you have come. And if you don't know where you are, you can't chart a course to determine where you are going. Understanding where you are, in a very accurate way—at any given time—is critical in navigating in a disruptive world.

This tradition of learning how to use a sextant reminded us how important and how difficult it can be to figure out where you are! If you know where you have come from and you know where you are, then it is much easier to know where you are going.

"Every decision you make—every decision—is not a decision about what to do. It's a decision about who you are. When you see this, when you understand it, everything changes. You begin to see life in a new way. All events, occurrences, and situations turn into opportunities to do what you came here to do."
Neale Donald Walsch

I've talked about being authentic throughout the book. It is very critical to be with and find people who are genuine and care about you. The people who care the most are those who allow you to find out who you truly are and allow you to be genuine. They accept it, support it, and encourage it. They might even inspire it. You have to be willing to do the same as you move through this disruptive world. You have to be supportive of and encouraging of everyone you encounter who is attempting to move forward. We are all in this together. You have to be genuine and sincere.

As I wrap up, I want to remind you of what I have talked about thus far.

- Be clear about your goals and objectives; have an outcome orientation.

- Bend your mind in critical and conceptual ways; see through clutter.

- Build an authentic and genuine team who want to see you do well—people who are nurturing your success.

- Always be prepared to move quickly. The perfect moment never comes. You have to move forward and act.

- Be passionate about what you believe in. Be emotionally engaged.

- Above all else, keep the faith—a strong faith will see you through.

"We won't get fooled again."
Pete Townsend, The Who

**"Take time to deliberate; but when
the time for action arrives,
stop thinking and go in."**
Napoleon Bonaparte

**"Good judgment comes from experience,
and a lot of that comes from bad judgment."**
Will Rogers

**"Success is not final, failure is not fatal. It is the
courage to continue that counts."**
Winston Churchill

Hot Wash Up:

CLARITY

Be clear about what you want. When you get clarity, you can do everything else that is required to move forward. Be absolutely and resolutely clear.

QUANTUM THINKING

Bend your perspective. Focus and pull disparate points together; look around and through the clutter. Don't believe the hype and don't get distracted by irrelevant information.

HYPER-COLLABORATION

Develop a personal strategy. Consider concepts you need to learn (and un-learn). Build a personal team that nurtures your success and wants you to succeed.

AGILITY

The 70 percent solution: Don't procrastinate; move forward; take kinetic action. Connect, communicate, and practice; adapt, overcome, and innovate; become comfortable being uncomfortable. Fall forward.

PASSION

Take required action. Build confidence to overcome; pay little attention to naysayers. If it was easy, anybody could do it!

FAITH

Keep a deep and enduring faith; if your faith is strong, it will sustain you. Strong faith enables you to push forward through obstacles. Faith is on your side—never give up and never surrender.

Suggested Reading

For a more extensive list of suggested media content,
please visit: www.jp3rd.com.

A Whole New Mind	Daniel H. Pink
The 8 Cylinders of Success	Jullien Gordon
Finding Your Element	Ken Robinson
The Global Achievement Gap	Tony Wagner
Rework	Jason Fried
Building on the Promise of Diversity	R. Roosevelt Thomas Jr.
Corps Business	David H. Freedman
Managing Differently	James Rodgers
Drive	Daniel H. Pink
Can We Talk about Race?	Beverly Tatum
The Heart & The Fist	Eric Greitens
The New Jim Crow	Michelle Alexander
Mindset: The New Psychology of Success	Carol Dweck
A History of Future Cities	Daniel Brook
The Dip	Seth Godin
Men We Reaped	Jesmyn Ward
Life's Operating Manual	Tom Shadyac
The End of Power	Moises Naim
The Post-American World	Fareed Zakaria
The Internal Enemy	Alan Taylor
John Henry Days	Colson Whitehead
Big Data	Viktor Mayer-Schonberger Kenneth Cukier
Blink	Malcolm Gladwell
Three Billion New Capitalists	Clyde Prestowitz
The Quest: Energy, Security, and the Remaking of the Modern World	Daniel Yergin
Thinking, Fast and Slow	Daniel Kahneman
Quiet	Susan Cain

Terminology

Billet: A specific job held by someone in a military unit.

Blue Water: Deep water or open ocean.

Carpe Diem: Seize the day; make the most of the present time.

Crossing the Line: Crossing the equator—traditional initiation ceremony where one goes from being a pollywog to a shellback.

DOD: The Department of Defense or the Pentagon. The branch of the US government directly in charge of US National Security and the US Armed Forces. It is the largest employer in the world and is headed by the Secretary of Defense (SECDEF). It is composed of three subordinate military departments: The Department of the Army, The Department of the Navy, and the Department of the Air Force.

Hot Wash or Hot Wash Up: Navy term for a summary or after-action report of lessons learned, usually from an exercise or training evolution.

JSC: Joint Chiefs of Staff

LPH: Landing Platform Helicopter: Large navy amphibious assault ship distinguished by full-length flight deck. Delivers marines via heli-borne assault.

NAVDEVGRU (Naval Development Group): *United States Naval Special Warfare Development Group often referred to as SEAL Team 6.* The mission of DEVGRU is classified, but is thought to include counterterrorism and high-value hostage rescue. In addition, its mission is thought to include testing of advanced naval warfare techniques and advanced equipment. Most information concerning DEVGRU is classified and details of its activities are not usually commented on by either the POTUS or the DOD.

NAVSPECWARCOM (Naval Special Warfare Command): Also known as NAVSOC or NSWC; group includes SEALs and Special Warfare Combatant Craft Crews (SWCC). They are the naval component of US Special Operations Command. NSWC provides doctrinal guidance and resources to ensure component maritime special operations forces are ready to meet the operational requirements of combatant commander.

Oiler: A combat logistics ship that replenishes other ships with fuel and in some cases food, mail, ammunition, and other necessities while at sea, in a process called underway replenishment or UNREP.

OOD: Officer of the deck. Direct representative of the commanding officer. Navy officer in charge of safely operating the ship during a defined watch period. The person on the bridge who is responsible for safely navigating and running the ship when underway at sea.

Salty: To be savvy or experienced. A term usually associated with the maritime professions and sailors.

Steamin' Machine or Steaming Machine: A navy ship that is moving with great speed. A navy ship that is disciplined, buttoned-up, and prepared for battle.

UA or Unauthorized Absence: Military term for being absent without leave (AWOL). The United States Navy and United States Marine Corps refer to this as UA. It can refer to a temporary or permanent desertion, depending on time away from unit or post.

USMC: United States Marine Corps

USN: United States Navy

About the Author

JP₃
Julius Pryor, III

Julius Pryor III is a **leading edge thinker**. He is a **speaker, author**, and **strategic consultant**. Julius conducts seminars for business schools, universities, corporations, the military, and government agencies. He speaks about conceptual innovation, being relevant in the twenty-first century, and becoming more comfortable being uncomfortable.

Julius develops kinetic strategies focusing on clarity of objectives and measurable outcomes. His work is grounded in understanding how organizational culture affects individual and team behavior. He emphasizes sustainable results in the workforce, workplace, and global marketplace.

He has held executive level jobs at Johnson & Johnson (J&J), Coca-Cola Enterprises (CCE), Russell Athletic, Abbott Labs, and Takeda Pharmaceuticals. He was the vice president of global diversity at both J&J and at CCE.

Julius is a US Navy captain, surface warfare officer, and certified instructor for the Navy Officer Leadership Development Program. He completed coursework at the Naval Postgraduate School and the National Defense University. He has held numerous leadership roles in the navy up to and including, executive officer, fleet staff officer, and unit commanding officer. He was in the re-commissioning crew of the USS *Missouri* (BB-63) and is one of a select few to have served as an active-duty **battleship turret officer**.

Julius is a **graduate of Morehouse College** and The Williston Northampton School (Easthampton, Massachusetts). While at Morehouse, he was initiated into Psi Chapter of the Omega Psi Phi Fraternity.

For more information about Julius Pryor III, his book,
or his upcoming events, please visit:
www.jp3rd.com.